ERUPTIVE PHENOMENA
AND GEOLOGY
OF
MONTE SOMMA & VESUVIUS

Number *eighty*

GEOLOGICAL MAP

OF

MONTE SOMMA & VESUVIUS,

CONSTRUCTED BY

H. J. JOHNSTON-LAVIS,

M.D., M.R.C.S., B.ès.S., F.G.S., etc.

DURING THE YEARS 1880-88.

Scale : 1 : 10000 (6·33 Inches = 1 Mile.)

A SHORT AND CONCISE ACCOUNT

OF THE

ERUPTIVE PHENOMENA & GEOLOGY

OF

MONTE SOMMA AND VESUVIUS

IN EXPLANATION OF THE

GREAT GEOLOGICAL MAP OF THAT VOLCANO,

Constructed during the years 1880 to 1888.

BY

H. J. JOHNSTON-LAVIS, M.D., M.R.C.S., B.ès.Sc.

*Fellow of the Geological Society of London ; Member of the Società Geologica
Italiana ; the Geologist's Association of London ; the Société Belge de
Géologie, Paléontologie et Hydrologie ; British Association for Advance-
ment of Science ; Società dei Microscopisti Italiani ; Società Americana
d'Italia ; Honorary Corresponding Member of the Scottish Geographical
Society ; etc.*

LONDON:
GEORGE PHILIP & SON, 32, FLEET STREET.
1891.

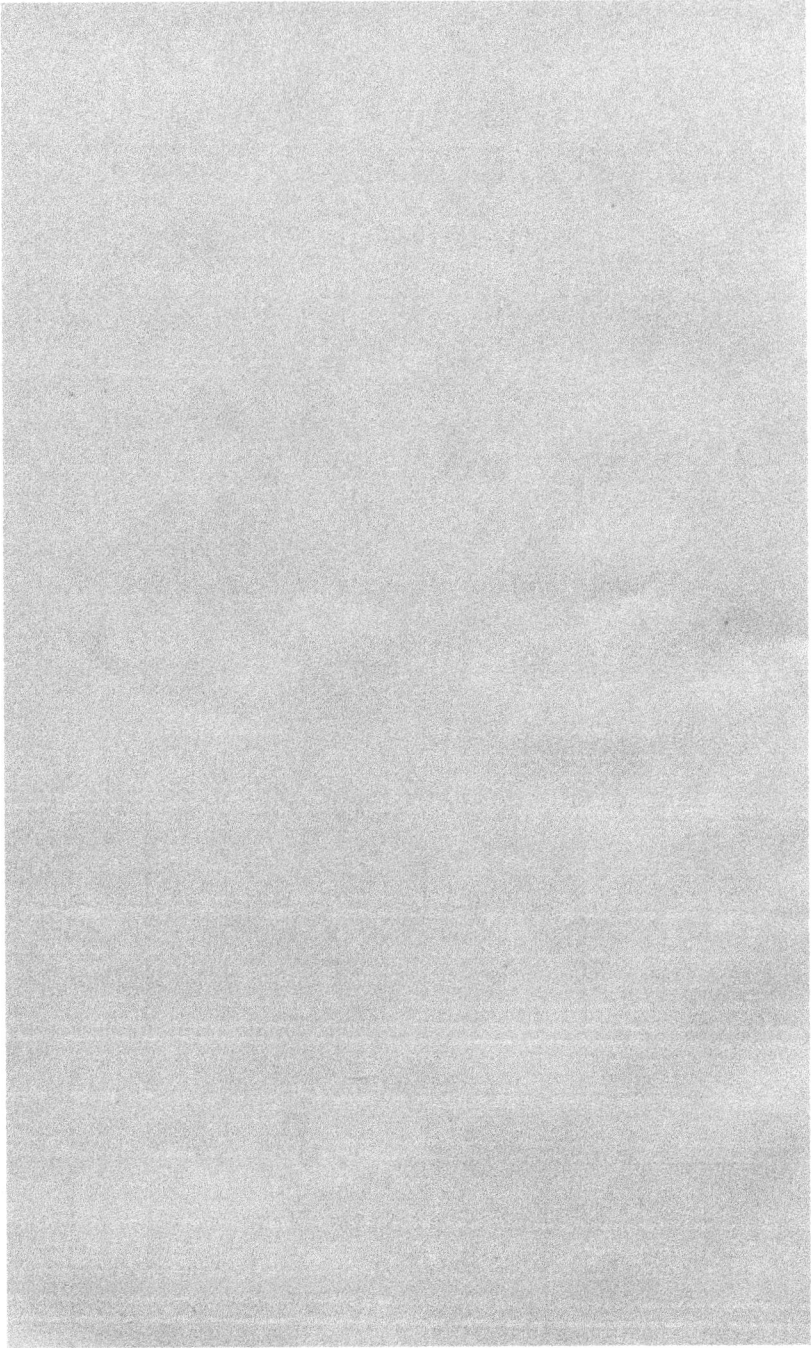

INTRODUCTION.

Vesuvius during many centuries has been looked upon as the type volcano, and although others have from time to time been ephemeral rivals, this great fire-vent of the Campanian plain still maintains its supremacy. Such can be explained as the consequence of a combination of several circumstances. In the first place, its situation, within easy access from one of the largest towns and sea-ports of the Mediterranean, so that there is no part of the mountain that cannot be visited and returned from in one day's excursion from Naples; the peculiar asymmetry in its shape, which, while being most striking, is very comprehensive; its beautiful lavas, pumices, fine escarpments, and numerous and varied dykes, combined with the extraordinary, very varied, and unique series of ejected blocks and their mineral contents, make it alike of profound interest to the mineralogist as to the physical geologist. Then again, its continuous activity has enticed the chemist to investigate its emanations with as much enthusiasm as that displayed by his scientific colleagues. Mineralogists, and perhaps still more, geologists, are keen connoisseurs of beautiful scenery, and have been seduced by the charms of the locality to pay more attention to the most important element in the beautiful land and sea-scape of the Gulf of Naples. Last, but not least, the innumerable reminiscences of history, and even romance, which bear engraven upon many pages the classic name of Vesuvius, which is known to almost every school boy or girl in the civilized world. Its great rival Etna, many times its size, possesses neither the bold slopes, finer precipices, or a more beautiful situation, whilst the rocks of the Sicilian volcano are monotonous in the extreme. Still less could the solitary, little varying Stromboli, or its equally insulated sister Vulcano, aspire to the majestic and elegant proportions or enviable position of type volcano which Vesuvius is likely to continue to hold.

Under such circumstances no apology is necessary for laying before the public a very detailed geological map of this unique volcano. No other geological Maps of Vesuvius have been published; the few physical maps already in existence are but of small scale, and based on defective topographical surveys, whilst their only aim has been a problematical delineation of the historic lava streams.

HISTORY OF THE MAP.

On taking up my residence in Naples, in 1879, my spare time was devoted to a study of the geological structure of Monte Somma and Vesuvius. Finding that amongst its extensive literature practically nothing had ever been written of the intimate structure of the volcano, I prepared to make an accurate survey of the whole mountain. The next two years were spent in investigating the general stratigraphical arrangement of the different deposits, with the special characters of each, the results of which were made public in a long memoir read before the Geological Society of London, and of course contains a more detailed account than can be included in the limited space at disposal in this short explanation of the map. The disentanglement of the complex stratigraphy, and its delineation in this large map, occupied my spare time till the end of 1888, and to facilitate the survey I took up my abode at different spots around the foot of the mountain. Of actual help I have received none, but rather obstruction, in some cases of a most regrettable nature, which, for the honour of science, had preferably remain undetailed. Of financial help, and above all, moral encouragement, I am deeply indebted to the "British Association for the Advancement of Science," which for six consecutive years have made small grants for the purpose of aiding in carrying out the work.

No doubt some errors have crept into such a work, a gigantic undertaking for a single individual, but everything has been done in a most conscientious manner. It must be mentioned also that most of the work has been prosecuted during the summer season, under a broiling and enervating Neapolitan sun; July, August, and September being my most free and, therefore, active months.

About 250 field days were required in the actual laying out of the map, not to speak of very numerous excursions of a preliminary or confirmatory character, so that not far from an actual year of my life, besides a considerable pecuniary outlay, has been spent in this difficult and arduous task.

My thanks are due, in the first place, to the landowners and peasants of the district, who universally allowed me free entry to their land; and although I was often troubled by excessive inquisitiveness, this never became objectionable when a little kind tact and diplomacy was adopted. Amongst many hundreds of the above whose possessions I have surveyed, there was but one who absolutely refused me admission to his property. Signor Catena seemed to either have fear of some diabolical act on my part, or was overruled by some exaggerated idea of his absolute power over his property, which pleased him to exert in an autocratic but ungracious or unintellectual manner, so that applications during six years remained infructuous in obtaining permission for a half-hour's visit to his fortunately limited domains. Any incorrectness in the mapping of the "Fagioneria" near Resina will be therefore comprehensive to the reader, as my only knowledge of the area was obtained by surreptitious peeps over the wall.

The various ways in which even very recent lavas become covered with soil suitable for the growth of vegetation, often attaining in a few years or even months to a very considerable depth, has necessitated a system of colouring which I believe to be novel—where the surface of the lava predominates, so far as area goes, over vegetable soil, the former is indicated by a scarlet tint with green crosses, which are given in three gradations of crowding, those nearest together representing the greatest amount of vegetable soil. Where vegetable soil predominates over the visible area of lava surface, a green tint is employed, covered by red crosses, the greater crowding of which indicates the more numerous projecting points and bosses of lava. When none of the latter appear at all, the limits of the lava stream are indicated by an interrupted vermillion line, the laying down of which gave a great amount of labour, and obviously in some cases is only approximately correct. As the plain scarlet tint indicates lava (in the case of the great Vesuvian cone also loose scoria, lapilli, sand, etc.) on which no vegetation beyond lichen has obtained a hold; it is therefore obvious that the gradual conversion of a rugged lava stream into a lovely garden or a fertile vineyard is represented by eight varieties of colouring. So many may at first sight appear superfluous, and I even commenced to use fewer, but experience taught me the necessity of having as many. The red ground, with green widest apart, corresponds to the appearance of a few broom bushes and some annuals in a few hollows or depressions of the lava, where a little dust or lapilli has been collected from the air or brought by water. The next stage generally corresponds to plantations of stone-pines or patches of lupins, with occasional fig trees. In the third stage, lupins, figs, with often vines and olives, are planted, whilst in the following stages almost any form of growth may be represented, according to the situation and caprice of the cultivator. The value of the other map tints will be given in the explanation of each deposit. It may, however, be mentioned here, that where different formations are exposed in steep sections, or over a very small area, they are necessarily marked in the map on a slightly exaggerated scale, but otherwise the shape and position of the exposures are indicated as clearly as possible.

The topographical map upon which the geological one is based, although very correct for most of the lower portions of the mountain, presents a few very gross errors amongst some of the higher valleys on M. Somma, and an endeavour has been made to correct them as well as possible in the geological map. Fortunately none of them occur where any important geological sections are exposed, and, therefore, they are worth no more than mention.

Where valleys exhibit important sections, and are not easily indicated, I have given them names to distinguish them in the future monograph of the mountain now in preparation. These names are chosen from amongst the most renowned vulcanologists, without distinction of nationality, many of whom were students of this volcano.

GENERAL DESCRIPTION.

ERA A.—The Campanian Plain, including what is now in part known as the Terra di Lavoro, formed in Pliocene times a great gulf, at present represented by those of Naples and Gaeta, near the northern end of which rose a limestone island of Monte Massico and a few other detached masses, and from which extended inlets amongst the calcareous Apennines. Against the cliffs of these the waves of the tertiary sea expended their fury, whilst sands and clays were laid down, and towards the end (?) of the Pliocene period numerous volcanic outbursts took place in the neighbourhood of Naples. Whether the vent around which Somma and Vesuvius were eventually piled up appeared before the first openings of the so-called Phlegrean Fields proper, is as yet undecided, and not unlikely to remain so. Probably, coincident with the earlier volcanic manifestations of the period, the shallow Pliocene sea bottom was raised to somewhere *near* its present level, and formed the fertile plains above-mentioned. What were the characters of the phenomena, or products of the first appearance of Somma-Vesuvius, we can only judge of by analogy. We may therefore suppose that the first materials ejected were pumices, which, either immediately or at a more distant period, were followed by lavas. Amongst the ejected blocks of M. Somma, basalts, trachytes, and other rocks not now seen *in situ* at this volcano, are met with; which fact may lead to one of two conclusions—either that amongst the earlier products of this focus the rocks occur, or that previous to, or during the earlier existence of Somma-Vesuvius, such products had been spread over its surface from neighbouring vents. Leucite, which is the dominant and characteristic silicate of the lavas, etc., of this volcano in its later stages, may have equally characterized the earlier products, should the above-mentioned rocks not be derived from this vent.

The plain which surrounds Somma-Vesuvius must be much higher relatively than when that volcano first manifested itself, for whilst a mountain grew up over 2100 m. or 7000 ft. in height, the surrounding district must also, in the absence of important rivers, have been raised by loose materials carried there through the air, or transported by water, as well as lava streams, some of which flowed great distances. Sections, in fact, confirm this, and show also that considerable additions were also being made by the ejecta of the neighbouring volcanic vents. Now the elevation of the Campanian Plain around the base of the mountain is not very great above the present sea-level, and also we have evidence that not long before the historic period the sea-level was relatively much higher than it actually is, as indicated by the Castellamare, and the Starza marine terraces. All these facts indicate that Vesuvius was originally an insular volcano. Most striking evidence, that proves it to have been much more than at present surrounded by comparatively deep sea, is the artesian well-boring at Ponticelli, where I found leucitic lavas, scoria, pumiceous, extending to a depth of 177·25 m. or 591 ft. The lavas were traversed from 59·90 m. or 200 ft. to 105·44 m. or 351 ft. from the surface, or 80·44 m. or 268 ft. from present sea-level; and if these really belong to Somma-Vesuvius a considerable inlet must have extended to near Pomigliano d'Arco sufficiently deep for the lavas to flow into. In well-borings at various localities around the foot of the mountain, confirmatory evidence of this kind has been met with; in fact, Breislak a century since arrived at a similar conclusion based on the latter evidence only.

Whether the leucitic pumices, pumiceous scoria, and scoria, met with in the boring at Ponticelli belong to the initiatory stage of the volcano, it is very difficult to determine; but at any rate they seem to prove explosive action at some period of its early history previous to the first outflow of the Somma lavas that are visible in the Atrio Sections.

During this early stage of activity, or not unlikely previous to it, occurred a gigantic explosive eruption of a grey trachytic dust and fragments of black scoria, which now constitute enormous well-marked deposits, extending over the whole Campanian Plain from Gaeta to Salerno, from Capri to Avellino and Benevento, and indistinctly represented at even much greater distances. This was ejected with all probability from a vent situated a short distance to the S.W. of Camaldoli of Naples, which produced at the same time the *piperno*, a more fluid homologue of the pipernoid tuff.

ERA B., PHASE I.—The more certain portion of the history of the Somma-Vesuvius volcano is that illustrated by the great section of the Atrio del Cavallo, where we see, for a height of 322 m. or 1073 ft., lavas, scorias, lapilli and dusts, piled one above another, and constituting one of the largest sections in Europe. All these lavas are comparatively basic, and contain leucite as a characteristic mineral, which ranges from microlitic up to beautiful crystals over 1 c.m. or $\frac{1}{2}$ in. in diameter. The other principal constituent minerals are magnetite and its allies, olivine, much augite, with basic felspars—anorthite, bytownite and labradorite. These represent in section part of the materials that were added to the great cone when it grew from about 600 m. or 2000 ft. to its maximum height of about 2100 m. or 7000 ft., and indicate a state of activity almost identical with the phenomena presented by Vesuvius from 1631 up to the present. At the end of that period the mountain must have presented the appearance of a beautiful symmetrical cone, about 2100 m. or 7000 ft. high, with the sweeping curves of its flanks only broken by parasitic cones, some of which can still be seen beneath the tuffs of Monte Somma. The whole of the Atrio section is traversed by numerous dykes, many of which no doubt reached the surface and supplied those parasitic cones and the resulting lava streams. Some of them are hollow, or, in other words, the central portion that was still fluid had been drained out from some parasitic cone at a lower level on the flanks of Somma. Some even have been refilled and emptied three consecutive times. The principal dykes are indicated as well as can be done on a flat map of a very steep section, and the numbers correspond to those painted in large figures in white paint on the actual dykes themselves.

All the fragmentary materials near the centre of the section are compressed and soldered together, no doubt in consequence of the original superincumbent weight of the cone and the high temperature near the old chimney.

All the deposits of this age, except the dykes—which are marked in violet lines—are indicated by a crimson tint.

ERA C, PHASE II.—The volcano then became dormant, so that vegetable soil was formed on its surface, and valleys excavated.

PHASE III., *Period* 1.—Pending that denudation progressed above, the stagnant magma beneath was gradually dissolving H_2O*, supplied from the surrounding rocks, until the tension rose to a point sufficient to overcome superincumbent obstacles, and an explosive eruption occurred, forming a crater which truncated the great cone. A very vitreous pumice of whitish colour, mixed with the débris of the summit of the cone, was spread over the surrounding country, as a thin but most persistent bed of from 0·10 to 1·00 m. or 4 to 40 inches.

Period 2.—Later, as the magma rose from deeper parts of the volcanic canal where it contained less H_2O, it cooled more slowly, consequently became darker in colour (chocolate brown), due to the formation of microlites and numerous crystals of extratelluric minerals, especially augite and magnetite dust, besides intratelluric materials that already existed in the paste, as felspars, amphibole, micas, etc. The thickness may attain as much as 4 m. or 5 yards, or more.

---

* H_2O is used, since it denotes no definite state of the compound, and is not confused with water or vapour, these latter terms being used when the compound exists as a separate entity, and not as a dissolved gas, as it is before vesiculation commences.

Period 3.—Superposed upon the last, but without any definite unconformity, are beds of fine rounded lapilli, in which the essential eruptive ejecta form the smallest portion, and consist of fragments of dense crystalline black pumiceous scoria, an exaggerated crystalline condition of the products of *Period* 2. The most important constituents of the deposit are rounded lapilli of dense leucitic lava, no doubt derived from the crater sides, ground up until small enough to be carried to the slopes of the volcano; and lastly, numerous yellow, much fumarolized fragments of similar rocks. The whole of this deposit attains a thickness of from about 0·80 m. or 2½ ft., to 4 m. or 13½ ft.

Period 4.—The last-described deposit sometimes passes up into, or may be represented by, a bed of very coarse leucitic breccia. This deposit is remarkably developed in the Vallone Pollena and Grande, above Massa di Somma, where the valley sides show a thickness of from 2 to 55 m. A purplish-brown dust encloses fragments of old lavas, scorias, or other constituents of the great cone; the blocks of the former often attaining some tons in weight. How these materials reach this particular slope of the volcano in such abundance cannot be determined. Two explanations suggest themselves—either they are alluvial, having issued by the lower lip, or a lateral baranco of the new formed explosion crater, and derived from its drainage, or represent the last explosive efforts of *Phase* III. from some later opening which may possibly be represented by the depression between I Canteroni, the Salvatore ridge, where stands the observatory, and the mass of Somma. The internal arrangement of the materials are rather against any alluvial origin. It must be remembered that the main explosive crater must have been much smaller than that represented by the present Atrio del Cavallo.

We learn from these deposits that Phase III. commenced with a violent explosion, which, after excavating a crater and covering the mountain slopes with a white, vitreous, and later by a denser, darker, more microcrystalline pumice, the explosive action was reduced to grinding up the materials of the crumbling in edges of the crater cliffs, and ejecting them as small fragments until probably the vent choked. Probably, after a short time, the obstructing materials were suddenly blasted out, forming Period 4. These different beds are represented on the map by a blue tint.

PHASE IV., V., *Periods* 1 *and* 2.—As I have elsewhere explained, the mechanism of eruptive action, the direct sequent of the above phenomena, should be the issue of the magma from the chimney, no longer so rich in vapour as to be fragmentary, but as continuous lava streams. It is the appearance of these lavas or the return of chronic activity which constitute a new phase. What repair took place to the crater of PHASE III. we know nothing, but it is not unlikely that an eruptive cone of considerable height was built up, though no lava streams seem to have overflowed the edge of the great crater, but radial dykes reached the flanks of the great cone, and burst forth, building up parasitic cones, from which streams of lava poured. Two of these eruptive apparatuses are well shown in plan on the map; that of the Val. San Severino, at an altitude of 375 m., and in the Val. Von Buch, where the eruptive cones are seen in section; and at a lower level of the slopes the lavas that issued from the same are exposed in numerous ravines, indicated in the map by a brown tint. These lavas differ from the older ones of Somma in that their felspar is in not inconsiderable part a sanidine or near ally, whilst leucite is nearly absent; and the lava, especially outflows, possesses a very fine vesicular structure, more of a pumiceous than a scoriaceous character. At the Val. San Severino two distinct lava-flows are superposed, the upper approaching much more the usual type, showing that the activity was still advancing towards the true Vesuvian character, and really representing two eruptive periods.

PHASE V.—What circumstances brought about a stage of repose in the volcano I can offer no suggestion, but that such repose did occur is proved by the numerous

deeply-weathered surfaces and vegetable soils, subsequent
to the last deposits, and antecedent to the ejection of new
eruptive materials.

PHASE VI., *Periods* 1, 2, 3, and 4.—The energy stored
up during the quiescence again resulted in explosive
eruptions, no less than four of which occurred consecu-
tively during PHASE VI. The description of each would
here occupy too much space, and for minuter details refer-
ence should be made to my original paper in the Quart.
Jour. Geol. Soc., Lond. Each eruption was characterized
by, first, the emission of lighter, whiter, more vitreous
pumice, with porphyritic enclosures of intratelluric or pre-
eruptive formed minerals, principally sanidine, amphibole
mica, and a little magnetite, followed as the eruption
progressed by more microlitic, denser, and darker varieties, with much pyroxene and magnetite dust, with
microlitic felspars, but *with no leucite*. These beds of
pumice contain also numerous fragments of old lavas,
scorias, etc., constituting the remains of the great cone
which was being eviscerated by a gradually enlarging
and deepening crater. The apex of this crater soon extended down below the limit of volcanic rocks into the
sub-volcanic platform, so that we find numerous fragments
of fossiliferous Pleistocene? calcareous conglomerate,
Pleistocene clays, mudstones, and sandstones in the
bottom of the deposits of *Period* 1, whilst the subjacent
baked limestones were reached towards the end of that
outburst. In later eruptions, especially that of *Period* 4,
the crater apex had extended down to the deeper-seated
limestones, often entirely converted into different sili-
cates or ultrabasic rocks, so as to graduate into the very
volcanic rocks that metamorphosed them. In fact these
accidental ejectmenta form a very important constituent
of the deposits. I have estimated that at the end of the
four eruptions the crater apex must have been 800 m.
below sea level.

The third and last material ejected in all these explosive eruptions is fine dust, which is produced in part by
the interstitial disintegration of the magma from the forming and escaping vapour, which, however, is then no

longer sufficiently powerful to project the materials, so that they could fall on the cone sides, except as fine dust. Some of the cooled magma, materials from the crumbling crater-walls, etc., are gravitating down to the crater apex, where, meeting the escaping vapours, they are by them churned and ground up and ejected from time to time as fine lapilli, sand or dust. These dust deposits are often met with on Monte Somma possessing a vesicular, pisolitic, concretionary, false-bedded or even resorted structure, due to the manner of mixing with more or less rain at the time of their deposition.

All these eruptions were pre-historic, with the possible exception of the last, about which some doubtful legends are sometimes quoted. Each one did much to progressively excavate an extensive crater within the heart of the great cone, truncating it to nearly one half of its original height. The limits of this crater extend from about the 650 m. contour line on the S. of the mountain, round the Val d'Inferno on the E., the eastern end of the Canteroni ridge on the W., and the great escarpment of Monte Somma on the N., that now overhangs its remains, now known as the Atrio del Cavallo. The great Atrio cliff section is part of the old crater wall, which may have slightly been re-pared by the first historic or plinian eruption. Some, if not all, of these outbursts occurred from an axis to the W. of S. of the one around which the old cone of Somma had been built—a very common occurrence in volcanoes. The reason of this displacement was in all probability the resistance offered by the old plug of cooled lava filling the chimney, and the greater height of superincumbent rock over the old axis of the cone, and the greater induration of its core. The crumbling in of the sides, and the materials washed down from them, soon filled up this great hollow nearly or quite to the level of the lower edge, in which state it was in the time of Strabo and Sparctacus. Some old wall paintings found at Pompeii show us the cone truncated obliquely, due, as I have said, to the eccentricity of the axis or axes of the explosive eruptions. It is to this ruin of the grand old cone that the name of Monte Somma is now applied and understood by geologists, which ruin corresponds to that portion of the mountain in existence up to the year A.D. 79.

PHASE VII., *period* 1.—In the year A.D. 63 a violent and destructive earthquake damaged to a great extent the town of Pompeii, and was followed by other shocks. In the month of November, A.D. 79, another explosive eruption burst forth destroying Pompeii, Herculaneum, Stabiæ, and numerous villages and country houses. The materials then ejected are very similar to those produced during the earlier explosive eruptions with the exception of one very important character, namely, that all the pumice contains microlitic leucite in considerable abundance, which not only is the case with this, but also with every subsequent eruption. We learn from Pliny's account that the wind was blowing from the N., so that the pumice deposits of this eruption are hardly recognizably represented N. of a line drawn E.W. through the Punta del Nasone, the highest point of Monte Somma, whilst it forms very important deposits to the S. of that line, and especially to the E., where great quantities fell upon the limestone mountains of the Sorrentine peninsula, although the culminant point M. Santangelo is 166 m. or 500 ft. higher than the present summit of Vesuvius, or 500 m. or about 1500 ft. above the lowest edge of the then crater rim. The characters of the ejectamenta can be beautifully studied in the streets of Pompeii, where they are separable into three divisions of 1st, white vitreous pumice, 2nd, darker microcrystalline pumice, 3rd, pumiceous ash, which is nearly always pisolitic. At Herculaneum these several materials mixed with others into one rather uniform paste, which has gradually consolidated into a more or less compact yellow tuff which attains a thickness of 20 m. or 60 ft. or more; whilst that over Pompeii rarely exceeds 8 to 10 m. or 25 to 30 ft., and often is much less. At Pompeii the regular arrangement and stratification indicates that the materials fell from the air, whilst those at Herculaneum obtained their present arrangement by the action of water collecting and transporting the materials down some baranco or valley.

It is probable that this eruption did little to enlarge

the original existing crater even at its commencement, and probably towards its end it built up a narrow low crater ring within the great Atrio crater, so laying the foundations of the new cone of Vesuvius.

PHASE VII., *periods 2 to 6.*—In the years A.D. 203, 243, 305, 321, 471 or 472, and 512, eruptions are recorded from Vesuvius. The long intervals between each, with no record of intervening chronic activity, point to these as being more nearly related to the explosive type of eruption, and therefore we should expect to find deposits of materials corresponding to such. At the Canale di Arena and many other spots such deposits do occur. The different beds differ very much, but all present certain common characters. In the first place the essential ejectamenta contains leucite in abundance, which mineral attains in these pumiceous scorias and scoriaceous pumices the greatest size and perfection, so that beautiful crystals nearly 3 c.m. in diameter are sometimes met with. The shorter intervals between the outbursts, and the more limited time allowed for the solution of H_2O, will account for this, as well as the denser, more microlitic and crystalline structure with a marked increase in size of all the extratelluric minerals and the presence of fewer sanidines and amphiboles. One bed actually is constituted by a very vesicular scoria. In my original memoir an attempt is made to correlate these deposits with some of the above mentioned eruptions.[*]

All the eruptions 1036-1038, 1049, 1138-1139, 1306, 1500, 1568 and probably many others not recorded, from what little is known of them were of the paroxysmal rather than explosive type. It is not unlikely that the main portion of their products were fragmentary, and went to build up the Vesuvian cone to what we see it as represented in engravings before 1631. In fact, the great development of cone and small crater indicate with certainty the faint disruptive power of these later outbursts. It is mentioned that in one or two of them lava flowed,

---

[*] Since writing the above evidence has been brought forward of an eruption in 780, and from the description lava flowed.

but it probably was confined within the so far unobliterated crater fosse between the new cone of Vesuvius and the Somma crater ring, (Atrio del Cavallo, Pedimentina etc.) These deposits of Phase VII., which are of no very great thickness, with the exception of those of the Plinian eruption *(Period 1)*, are indicated on the map by the green tint which also includes a very small quantity of surface material of still later date.

ERA D, PHASE VIII.—In 1631 occurred one of the most terrible eruptions of Vesuvius. It was not of the explosive but of the paroxysmal type, and besides the fragmentary materials, consisting of scoria, lapilli, sand, and numerous large streams of lava poured down the slopes of the volcano, burning up in their course and burying towns and villages, with a great destruction of life. Since that date the volcano has never become thoroughly dormant for any length of time. Generally, the volcanic activity consists of constant varying, but feeble explosions at the main vent, with often small dribbling of lava from some lateral opening near the summit of the great cone. This state is interrupted from time to time by paroxysmal eruptions, which are due to the formation of radial dykes which extend from the main chimney outwards to the slopes of the cone ; then as much of the lava as there is in the central canal above the level of the new vent escapes, thus immediately lightening by so much the pressure on the remainder in the chimney below, which lava, consisting of a liquid holding a quantity of gas in solution proportionate to the original pressure, froths up and issues forth after the first gushes. It follows, therefore, other influences apart, that the outpour of lava is in direct proportion to the vertical distance between the original height of the lava column and the level of the new lateral opening. Series of parasitic craterets are indicated by yellow bands on the vermillion tint of the map. The principal ones now visible, of which the dates of their formation are known, are those formed at the eruptions of 1760, 1794, and 1861. The largest parasitic cone, however, is Camaldoli della Torre, which is certainly of considerable antiquity, as the monastery built on its summit dates from an earlier period than 1631. I have never found any evidence that could fix its date except the following :—On the coast opposite there crops out a peculiar and unique fine vesicular lava which is covered by some remnants of the pumice beds of Phase VI. The resemblance of this lava to that of Phase IV., the fact that it is earlier than Phase VI., make it not improbable that it may be of the age of the former. In a well recently dug at the foot of the Camaldoli cone, scoria, much like the abovementioned lava, was obtained, and it may therefore be suggested that they both issued here. All therefore that can be said is that *probably* Camaldoli is referable in age to Phase IV. The Fossa della Monaca, a deep conical hollow bordered by a low scoria rim, stands just above a lava-cake and scoria cone, called Bocca il Viulo. They both appear comparatively fresh, and although their date is not known, there is some evidence to show that they mark one of the points from which issued part of the lava in the 1631 eruption.

The lavas of PHASE VIII. differ little from those of Monte Somma—the larger streams are generally of finer grain, because they have come from great depths and have issued more quickly, whilst the smaller streams that dribble near the top of the cone are characterized by larger crystals, especially of leucite, consequent on the long time allowed for crystallization whilst the magma is simmering in the top of the chimney. For the same reason the larger streams are generally very rough and scoriaceous on their surfaces, whilst the shorter ones tend to have a corded surface, as their contained H_2O, had, to a great extent, been boiled off before they flowed. The same arrangement and characters can be traced in the ancient lavas of Somma, only they often appear to be more leucitic, since that mineral from its more advanced decomposition is whiter and more obvious. The lavas of Phase VIII., or from 1631 onwards, are, as already mentioned, coloured vermillion. This same colour is also used for the scoria and lapilli of the great Vesuvian cone of Vesuvius, as the intermingling of these with lava of the same age is so intricate that they could not be mapped, and even if they could, it would be a useless labour, as changes and additions are constantly going. At the S.E. foot of the cone it has been necessary to draw an artificial boundary, and this is indicated for the short distance, where necessary, by a serrated junction of the green and vermillion tint.

During the recent phase of Vesuvius dense black lapilli have been spread over the slopes of the volcano for considerable distances, and form deposits of no mean thickness. As we recede from the eruptive axis of Vesuvius the deposits of these lapilli thin out, so that there is no definite boundary line. I have, however, attempted to indicate, by the red dots on green, the area where these lapilli form an important constituent of the surface soil. The great screen of Somma seems to have confined their distribution to the N., and they extend much farther to the E. than the W., probably due to strong winds in that direction pending some of the great eruptions. The valleys and ravines on the E.N.E. slopes of Mt. Somma are thickly clothed with them, so that few of the older deposits are visible.

SURFACE EROSION.

The sides of Monte Somma are scored by deep valleys and ravines, which were in great part cut out before the old Somma cone was truncated down to its present level, as the valley depressions extend up to and notch the culminant ridge, forming a series of serrations. Physically each valley may be divided into three sections :—the upper third is the steepest but shallowest, and is chiefly engaged in the collecting of water which it empties into the middle section, where, from a slightly diminished inclination, and the great head of the water, erosion progresses with great violence, cutting out deep and narrow ravines. As the stream descends, its energy has been gradually expended ; it is charged with enormous quantities of solid matter (often 15 to 20 per cent.), and on reaching the lower third of the valley where the incline is slight, its speed is diminished, and it deposits much of its burden and flows on ; but a large part also sinks into the porous soil.   In consequence of this the solid materials, which it has already deposited forms a dejection, cone, or alluvial fan, which eventually blocks its course, so that the stream eventually has to cut its way through this cone, forming a lowly-inclined and vertical cliff-sided valley, locally called a *Lagno*, whilst the upper portions are called *Vallone*. The result of all this is that the upper section of the valley is almost uneroded, the middle section loses much material, and therefore lowers the mountain surface at those levels, whilst the toe of the slope is pushed out on the plain, so that the volcanic cone assumes a concave slope not due to subsidence, as is sometimes supposed to be the case.   Whilst the valley is being excavated in the soft materials, these crumble away and leave sloping banks, but when the old lava streams are reached, the sides there remain perpendicular, so that the *Vallone* would then show a Y shaped section.   When erosion extends down and through the lava beds which alternate with scoria and other fine materials, the valley bottom gets broken up into steps from the lava beds, resisting erosion and remaining as ledges, which of course much impedes any further rapid excavation.   All these valleys are for the most part of the year quite dry, and it is only when the downpour of rain is so rapid that the percolation into the ground is exceeded that these valleys become water, or more properly mud or *moya* courses.

Along the intervening ridges the usual foot and mule-paths are made, and on account of the incoherent nature of the more recent deposits (Phases III., IV., V., VI., VII., and VIII.) the vegetation shield of these gets cut into, and gives rain and wind a fair start, which soon converts them into deep narrow trenches, often not more than 3 or 4 m. broad and 10 or more m. deep.   This form of valley, for it eventually becomes one, is called locally a *Cupa*.

During different great eruptions the valleys have been choked by the ejecta, and again cut out afresh, sometimes along a new axis.   The Vallone di Pollena is a good example of this, and a section of it to scale may be consulted in my original paper.

Want of space has limited this description, rendering it very sketchy, but it must be remembered its only object is to give the reader an idea of the principal facts indicated in the map. Those requiring further details for the time being may conveniently refer to the following papers.

Phillips, J.—*Vesuvius*, 1868.

Lobley, J. L.—*Mount Vesuvius*, 2nd edition, London, 1889.

Johnston-Lavis.—*The Geology of Monte Somma and Vesuvius, being a Study in Vulcanology*: Quart. Jour. Geol. Soc., London, 1884, vol. XL., p. 35-112, 2 wood-cuts and 1 chromo plate. *The Relationship of the Structure of Igneous Rocks to the Conditions of their Formation*: Sc. Proceed. R. Dublin Soc., 1886, vol. V., N.S., p. 112-156. *On the Form of Vesuvius and Monte Somma*: Geol. Mag., Dec. 3, vol. V., p. 445-451, fig. 1.

www.ingramcontent.com/pod-product-compliance
Lightning Source LLC
Chambersburg PA
CBHW081453070426
42452CB00042B/2724